paul and jeanne rankin

HOT FOOD

paul and jeanne rankin

HOT FOOD

photography by
James Merrell

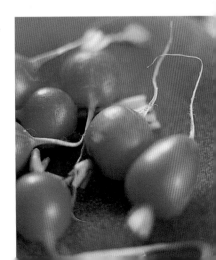

MITCHELL BEAZLEY

Art Director: **Jacqui Small**

Executive Art Editor: **Penny Stock**

Executive Editor: **Susan Haynes**

Editor: **Sasha Judelson**

Photography: **James Merrell**

Food preparation: **Paul Rankin**

Stylist: **Sue Skeen**

Home Economist: **Jane Stevenson**

The publishers would like to thank Maryse Boxer, Chez Joseph and the
Designers Guild for the glass and china.

First published in Great Britain in 1994 by Mitchell Beazley
an imprint of Reed International Books Limited
Michelin House, 81 Fulham Road
London SW3 6RB
and Auckland and Melbourne

Reprinted 1997

ISBN 1 84000 041 4

Colour reproduction by Rival Colour Limited, UK
Printed and bound by Cayfosa, Barcelona

contents

introduction

hot food

We adore spicy food, and this book brings together some of our favourites, many of which were discovered at memorable meals that we have shared and enjoyed during the time we circumnavigated the globe, in what we fondly remember as our "travelling years".

There is no doubt about it, the acceptance and enjoyment of hot food, be it pleasantly subtle or undeniably brash, is on the increase. Spice adds zest and zing, verve and vigour; with it, food becomes alive and jumps up off the plate.

Chances are, the ubiquitous curry was your introduction to hot food. For years the cuisines of India and China were synonymous with spicy foods. Nowadays there are a multitude of alternatives available right on our doorstep - Thai and Vietnamese, TexMex and Southwest, Mexican and Central American, Caribbean and African cuisines, all characterised by the exuberant use of chillies and other interesting spices.

Asian supermarkets and certain delicatessens have all the condiments used to create hot food. With a huge variety of oils and pastes, powders and flakes, dips and sauces, they are the perfect starting point for the uninitiated to begin their discovery of hot food. A spoonful of chilli oil tossed into a bowl of plain pasta is a perfect example of how a rather bland basic background, can be enhanced by a fiery flavour.

Hot food is spontaneous food. The best tastes come from the freshest foods, so buy and prepare as late as possible. The spring onions, chillies, garlic and herbs chopped just before you use them will have miles more flavour than something you have had waiting around for hours. Both metric and imperial measurements have been given in all recipes. We suggest you use either metric or imperial, not a mixture. Eggs should be size 2, milk full fat and use the freshest herbs you can find, unless otherwise stated, if you can't find fresh herbs use dried herbs as an alternative but halve the quantities stated. Ovens should be preheated - if you are using a fan assisted oven, follow the manufacturer's instructions for adjusting the time and the temperature.

Hardly any of the recipes within *Hot Food* are mouth blistering; most are delicate in their balance of piquancy and flavour. Some recipes are instantly loveable, others are an acquired appreciation. From robust soups to elegant canapés, from easy snacks to sophisticated dinner parties and everyday dishes, the range of recipes varies in the degree of heat; there are dishes to suit all palates and all occasions.

So get pepped up, add some hot food and some cool jazz to your life. The only way is up.

Paul and Jeanne

canapés

spicy
chicken and prawn toasts

A fantastic little party appetizer, guaranteed to be a real hit so make a little extra. It also seems to be a great dish for introducing children to oriental-style tastes, just tone down the spicing somewhat, and chances are they'll even want to give you a hand in the preparation.

185 g (6 oz) peeled prawns

250 g (8 oz) lean chicken meat, cut into strips

2 egg whites (or just 1 egg)

1 clove garlic, chopped

½ tablespoon fresh ginger, chopped

2 tablespoons fresh coriander, chopped

2 scallions, sliced quite finely

1 tablespoon fish sauce

½ teaspoon salt

½ teaspoon freshly ground black pepper

8 slices stale white bread, crusts removed

black and white sesame seeds, vegetable oil for frying

In a food processor, mince the prawns and chicken with the egg. Process thoroughly until you have a coarse mince, occasionally clean the sides of the bowl with a spatula. Add the remaining ingredients, except for the bread, oil and sesame seeds. Process until you have an even paste-like mixture.

Spread the mixture onto the slices of bread, making sure that the mixture is evenly distributed. Sprinkle each slice with a few sesame seeds, and cut into 4 triangles. Heat the oil in a deep fat fryer, wok or large frying pan to about 180°C (350°F), or until a cube of bread browns in 30 seconds. Fry the triangles a few at a time, prawn and chicken side down, for 2-3 minutes or until crispy and brown.

Drain on kitchen paper and keep warm while you finish the rest. Serve as soon as possible.

Makes 32

chilli

garlic lamb in filo pastry

These tasty samosa-like snacks are miles ahead of the type of stuff that comes out of many a local Indian take-away. More reminiscent of good Indian home cooking, they are really worthwhile. Serve by themselves as canapés, or with a little salad and a light yogurt sauce for a first course.

In a heavy frying pan melt the butter, add the onion and fry over a moderate heat until soft and light brown. Add the mince, along with the raisins, garlic, chillies, ginger, turmeric, nutmeg and a little salt, and fry for 3-4 minutes. Add the water and cover, continue to cook gently for another 15 minutes, stirring occasionally. Uncover and cook for a few more minutes to evaporate any excess liquid, the mixture should be moist but not runny.

Remove from the heat, cool, and add the garam masala, coriander, salt and pepper and lemon juice.

To assemble, work with one or two sheets of filo pastry at a time, keeping the rest covered with a damp cloth to keep them from drying out.

Cut each sheet in half lengthwise, and then fold each piece in half lengthwise again to give 2 long narrow strips. Put a dollop of the mince mixture in one corner of each strip of pastry. Brush the pastry all over with the ghee (or melted butter) and fold the pastry and filling over at right angles to make a triangle. Continue folding in this way along the strip of pastry to form a neat triangular parcel. Brush all over with ghee, and put on a greased baking sheet. Repeat the process until all 12 parcels are made up. Place in a preheated oven 180°C (350°F), Gas Mark 4, for 10 minutes, then brush again with the remaining ghee and return to the oven for a further 5 minutes. While the parcels are cooking mix together all the ingredients for the yogurt sauce, if you are using it. Allow the parcels to cool a little before serving.

Makes 12

For the stuffing:

1 tablespoon butter

4 tablespoons chopped onion

200 g (7 oz) lean minced lamb

1 tablespoon raisins

3 cloves garlic, finely chopped

2 fresh green chillies,

deseeded and finely sliced

1 tablespoon ginger, chopped

¼ teaspoon turmeric

pinch of nutmeg

pinch of salt

2 tablespoons water

¼ teaspoon garam masala

1 tablespoon coriander leaves,

chopped

salt and freshly ground

black pepper

1 teaspoon lemon juice

For the pastry:

6 sheets of filo pastry

60 g (2½ oz) ghee, or melted

butter

For the yogurt sauce (optional):

6 tablespoons natural yogurt

1 tablespoon tomato ketchup

1 tablespoon chopped mint

marinated beef kebabs with a szechuan dipping *sauce*

This versatile dish can be a starting point for creating your own favourite recipe. Substitute the beef with chicken, lamb, or pork and serve with a salad as a starter or main course. If you are feeling creative try different marinades and sauces as well.

500 g (1 lb) sirloin or fillet steak

2 tablespoons vegetable oil

Marinade:

1 clove garlic, finely chopped

1 tablespoon brown sugar or honey

1 tablespoon dark soy sauce

1 teaspoon freshly ground black pepper

1 teaspoon curry powder

1 tablespoon vegetable oil

Dipping sauce:

2 tablespoons light soy sauce

2 tablespoons rice wine vinegar

1 tablespoon chopped ginger

½ tablespoon chopped garlic

½ teaspoon sugar

½ teaspoon freshly ground black pepper

4 teaspoons toasted sesame oil

1 teaspoon chilli sauce (or 2 fresh green chillies, deseeded and chopped)

2 spring onions, finely chopped

Mix together all the ingredients for the marinade in a small bowl. Cut the beef into 1 cm (½ inch) cubes and toss in the marinade. Allow to marinate for at least 15 minutes. Thread the cubes on to skewers or cocktail sticks, you should end up with 25-30 mini kebabs.

Mix together all the ingredients for the dipping sauce, except the spring onions, and reserve. The spring onions should be added at the last minute, just prior to serving.

In a heavy pan, heat the vegetable oil until almost smoking. Add the kebabs and sauté on all sides until nicely browned, this takes about 2 minutes. Add the spring onions to the dipping sauce, serve with the kebabs which should be as warm as possible.

Serves 6-8

kick ass

olives

These delicious little treats should always be on hand. Use them to accompany drinks, as appetizers, throw them into pasta dishes, on pizzas, or almost anything else you take a fancy to.

1 x 300 g (10 oz) tin of good quality olives (can be green or black, as desired)

Marinade:

1-2 teaspoons dried red chilli flakes

½ clove garlic, finely chopped

1 teaspoon ground coriander seeds

1 teaspoon caraway seeds

1 teaspoon dried mint

30 g (1 oz) preserved lemons, finely chopped

4 tablespoons water

4 tablespoons olive oil

Simply gently heat all the marinade ingredients together in a small saucepan until the mixture comes to a simmer. Allow to cool, and then in a small bowl, mix the marinade with the olives. Store in a jar in the refrigerator for at least 2 days to bring out the flavours.

steak tartare with sun-dried tomato

rouille

This is our up-to-date version of a great classic. To Paul, steak tartare always conjures up images of a bygone era...dinner clubs, tuxedos, elegant women and maybe even the sweet sound of jazz.

Make sure the beef is free from fat and sinews and then cut it into 1 cm (½ inch) strips. Place the strips into a chilled food processor bowl. Add all the seasoning ingredients, and process until the beef is nicely chopped to a fine mince (but not puréed). To make the rouille, combine the chillies, garlic, saffron, bread, egg, sun-dried tomatoes and salt in a blender or food processor and process just until you have a coarse purée. Slowly add the oil, with the blender still running, until the mixture thickens to a mayonnaise-like consistency. (If the mixture separates, add 1-2 tablespoons of boiling water and continue processing.) Add some freshly ground black pepper, taste for seasoning and scrape into a clean bowl.

For the croûtons, slice the baguette into thin rounds, lightly brush with olive oil and crisp in a preheated oven 170°C (325°F), Gas Mark 3, for approximately 5 minutes or until lightly browned. To serve, spoon the tartare mixture on to the cooled croûtons, top with a little rouille and serve.

Makes 24

450 g (14 oz) lean beef, can be sirloin, rump or fillet

2 shallots, finely chopped

4 anchovy fillets, chopped

1 teaspoon Dijon mustard

2 tablespoons fresh lemon juice

½ tablespoon chopped parsley

½ teaspoon freshly ground black pepper

1 teaspoon salt

½ teaspoon Tabasco sauce

For the rouille:

2 large dried chillies

3 cloves garlic, finely sliced

pinch saffron

2 slices of bread, crusts removed, and soaked in 8 tablespoons milk

1 egg

12 halves sun-dried tomatoes, roughly chopped

125 ml (4 fl oz) olive oil

125 ml (4 fl oz) vegetable oil

¼ teaspoon salt

freshly ground black pepper

For the croûtons:

1 thin baguette

4 tablespoons light olive oil

crispy
vegetable spring rolls with thai hot and sour sauce

Everyone loves spring rolls but it is quite difficult to find good vegetarian ones. These are light, zippy and tasty. It's fine to use dried or other fresh mushrooms if you can't find fresh shiitake mushrooms.

4 tablespoons vegetable oil

1 tablespoon finely minced garlic

1½ tablespoons finely minced fresh ginger

¼ white cabbage, very finely sliced

2 tablespoons grated carrot

10 shiitake mushrooms, finely sliced

1 tablespoon soy sauce

2 spring onions, finely sliced

120 g (4 oz) salted peanuts, roughly chopped

1 tablespoon toasted sesame oil

salt and pepper

30 spring roll wrappers

1 tablespoon cornflour

2 tablespoons water

oil for deep frying

Dipping sauce:

200 ml (7 fl oz) rice wine vinegar

4 tablespoons sugar

2 cloves garlic, finely chopped

2 small red chillies, finely chopped

1 tablespoon fresh coriander, for garnish

Heat the vegetable oil in a wok or large frying pan until smoking, quickly brown the garlic and ginger until they are aromatic. Toss in the cabbage, carrot and mushrooms. Fry for about 30 seconds to a minute, just until the cabbage is starting to wilt. Tip the cabbage mixture into a large bowl, and add the soy sauce, spring onions, peanuts and sesame oil. Mix together and taste for seasoning, add a little salt and pepper as needed.

To fill the spring rolls, put a level tablespoon of the mixture in the bottom corner of each wrapper. Blend together the cornflour and water and then brush the whole wrapper with the blended corn-flour/water mixture. Fold the bottom corner over the filling and then the left and right corners inwards, complete the spring roll by rolling it snugly shut.

For the hot and sour dipping sauce, combine the vinegar and sugar in a saucepan, stir over the heat until the sugar is dissolved. Bring to the boil and simmer uncovered for 5 minutes to mellow the vinegar, it should be reduced by half. Now add the garlic and chilli, and allow to cool.

Deep fry the rolls in hot oil - 180°C (350°F) or until a piece of bread browns in 30 seconds - until well browned. Drain on absorbent paper. Serve hot with bowls of the dipping sauce garnished with the freshly chopped coriander.

Makes 30 rolls

snacks

camembert quesadillas with papaya

salsa

Quesadillas must be one of the most popular Mexican dishes around. Most often these are served with tomato salsa and guacamole, but here is a delightful new salsa to try, easy to whip up and kid friendly too, at least in our household.

6 large flour tortillas (20-25 cm/8-10 inches)
300 g (10 oz) Camembert (not too ripe), cut into ½ cm (¼ inch) strips
1 tablespoon butter
1 tablespoon vegetable oil

For the salsa:
1 small red onion, finely chopped
500 ml (17 fl oz) boiling water
2 ripe papayas, peeled, sliced and cut into 1 cm (½ inch) dice
juice of 2 limes
1 large red chilli, deseeded and finely chopped
1 small green chilli (serrano), deseeded and finely chopped
50 ml (2 fl oz) light olive oil
1 tablespoon chopped mint
salt and freshly ground black pepper
salad or herb leaves (optional)

Prepare the quesadillas by simply covering three of the tortillas with the Camembert slices. Top each with one of the remaining three tortillas and set aside for the moment.

To make the salsa, first scald the red onion by pouring the boiling water over it. Then immediately drain the onion through a sieve. Now combine all the other salsa ingredients and allow the flavours to combine for at least ½ hour before using.

To cook, warm a large frying pan over moderate heat. Melt the butter with the vegetable oil in a separate dish. Brush the pan with this mixture, and then place the cheese tortilla in the pan. Cook for about 2 minutes on each side, or until golden brown. Keep the quesadillas warm in a low oven while you continue to cook the others. Cut each quesadilla into 4-6 wedges, and serve as soon as possible. Arrange on the plates with a good scoop of the papaya salsa and a few salad or herb leaves.

Serves 6

spicy glazed pecans

A snack with a kick, definitely destined to get you hooked. If you don't want to make this with pecans try using walnuts or hazelnuts instead. Any of these nut varieties will retain their own flavouring which is just enhanced by the glaze.

1½ tablespoons butter
3 tablespoons sugar
1 teaspoon salt
1½ teaspoons black pepper
½ teaspoon chilli powder
1 tablespoon water
225 g (7½ oz) pecan halves

Melt the butter in a heavy-based frying pan over a moderate heat. Add all the other ingredients, except the pecans, and stir until dissolved and bubbling. Add the pecans and stir constantly, be sure to coat all the pecans. Continue to cook for another 5-10 minutes, until the pecans are starting to caramelize, and are dried and crispy looking. Cool by spreading out on a baking sheet. Store in an airtight container.

Shown on page 18

piquant **popcorn**

Another really moreish snacking food, a great change from the usual salted type. Be sure to have plenty of cool drinks at hand, they'll be asked for!

50 g (2 oz) butter
1 teaspoon salt
½ teaspoon chilli flakes (optional)
½ teaspoon cracked black pepper
½ teaspoon ground cumin
½ teaspoon curry powder, (hot)
1 tablespoon chopped fresh ginger
1 clove garlic, finely chopped
3 tablespoons vegetable oil
125 g (4 oz) popcorn, still unpopped of course

In a small saucepan, melt the butter and add all the seasonings. Do not let this mixture fry, but keep it very hot.

In a large heavy bottomed saucepan heat the vegetable oil over a very high heat until it is nearly smoking. Add the corn, and shake. Wait until you hear the first few pops, then quickly toss in the spiced butter, cover and shake. Shake the pot continuously in a front to back motion until the corn stops popping. Quickly tip into an attractive serving bowl and munch out!

Shown on page 18

spicy goat's cheese and avocado
bruschetta

This is the type of snack you won't tire of. It is a healthy and natural food and yet can be elegant and extremely satisfying.

Arrange the slices of baguette on a baking sheet, and brush lightly with the olive oil. Bake in a preheated oven 190°C (375°F), Gas Mark 5, until crisp and lightly browned. Remove from the oven, and rub each slice twice with the garlic clove. Reserve these. To make the topping, cut the avocados in half and remove the stones. Hold the avocado skin side down in your hand, and cut the flesh into 1 cm (½ inch) cubes without breaking the skin. Now squeeze the skin and the diced flesh will pop out easily. Continue with each avocado, collecting the flesh in a medium-sized bowl.

Toss the avocado with the lemon juice (this prevents discolouration as well as adding flavour). Now also toss in the goat's cheese, tomato, thyme, chilli and a few drops of Tabasco (this is a personal thing, either you go for lots or only a little). Stir this briefly and taste to check the seasonings. Add more if desired. Spread each bruschetta generously with the mixture. Serve on a tray as a snack, or with a few rocket leaves tossed in vinaigrette as a starter.

Makes 16

½ **baguette, cut into ½ cm (¼ inch) slices**

100 ml (3½ fl oz) olive oil

1 clove garlic

4 ripe avocados

juice of 1 lemon

150 g (5 oz) goat's cheese log (at room temperature), peeled and crumbled

2 plum tomatoes, peeled, deseeded and roughly chopped

1 teaspoon fresh thyme leaves

1 large red chilli, deseeded and finely chopped

a few drops of Tabasco sauce

freshly ground black pepper

heuvos

rancheros

This is actually a Mexican version of that old stand-by, breakfast bacon and eggs. It can easily be enjoyed anytime. Both the beans and the rancheros sauce keep very well in the refrigerator, and so can be prepared days in advance. Incidently, both are fantastic with grilled chicken or pork.

200 g (7 oz) black turtle (or pinto) beans

2 cloves garlic, lightly crushed

1½ litres (2½ pints) water

2 tablespoons vegetable oil

1 small onion, finely chopped

1 small clove garlic, finely chopped

½ kg (1 lb) plum tomatoes, peeled, deseeded and chopped

2 fresh green chillies, deseeded and sliced

1-2 tablespoons barbecue style ketchup (smokey stuff, optional)

8 flour tortillas

Simmer the beans in a large pot with the garlic and water until soft, and just beginning to split. Season with salt and pepper and keep warm.

In a large pan heat the vegetable oil over a moderate heat, add the onion and garlic and fry gently for about 5 minutes, until the onion is soft. Now add the tomatoes, together with the chilli and barbecue sauce. Cook for about 5 more minutes, until you have a soft yet chunky sauce.

Warm the tortillas by piling them onto a plate, cover with cling-film and heat for 2 minutes at 50% of your microwave full power or alternatively heat them gently under the grill. Melt the butter in a non-stick pan and fry the eggs, the way you like them.

To serve, fold the tortillas in half, and set on the edge of a warm plate. Spoon some rancheros sauce and black beans beside the tortilla and then the eggs next to that. Top the beans with a little sour cream, and sprinkle with the fresh coriander and red onion.

Serves 4

1 tablespoon butter

8 eggs

Garnish:

4 tablespoons sour cream

2 tablespoons freshly chopped coriander

½ red onion chopped

salt and pepper

soups

chicken

noodle soup with peanuts and chilli

When will we here in the West learn from the East that this is the real fast food? Noodle soups are not only fast, but low fat, easy to digest, healthy, satisfying and very versatile. To be enjoyed to the maximum they should be eaten piping hot with great gusto and lots of slurping and sucking noises - this is the proper etiquette in the East! Have to hand a small bowl of chilli oil or chilli sauce, to be passed around at the table.

1 tablespoon vegetable oil
300 g (10 oz) boneless,
skinless chicken fillets
2 garlic cloves, finely chopped
1½ litres (2½ pints)
chicken stock
1 tablespoon sugar
2 tablespoons salted peanuts,
roughly chopped
2 spring onions, finely sliced
175 g (6 oz) fine egg noodles,
cooked, refreshed in cold
water and drained
6 leaves lettuce (preferably
Cos), shredded
2 tablespoons fresh coriander,
chopped
salt (optional)
soy sauce (optional)

Heat the oil in a large saucepan. Meanwhile cut the chicken into smallish dice or slices. Add the garlic to the hot oil and fry until lightly browned. Add the chicken and fry gently for another 2 minutes, until the meat stiffens. Add the chicken stock and sugar and bring to a gentle simmer and cook for 10 minutes.

At this stage, prepare your warmed soup bowls and call everyone to the table. To serve, divide the peanuts and spring onions equally among the bowls, and then add the remaining ingredients to the chicken broth.

Taste for seasoning, and add a little soy sauce or salt if needed. Divide the soup into the bowls, and serve with the chilli sauce or oil on the side, if you are using it. Those indulging would probably appreciate bibs!

Serves 6

Shown on page 26

lentil soup with roast

cumin

It's just great to see lentils being used more and more these days. They have truly become a super food, being cheap, healthy and versatile. Cumin is a heady spice which is soft, yet pungent, with a little kick at the end. If it's not spicy enough for you, simply add a few chopped chillies just prior to serving.

In a large saucepan sauté the onion, garlic and 3 teaspoons of the cumin in 2 tablespoons of the oil for about 5 minutes, letting the onion brown, and the cumin roast slightly.

Add the lentils, bay leaf, oregano and chicken stock. Bring to the boil and simmer for about 35 minutes or until the lentils are soft. Remove the bay leaf, and purée the soup in a blender. You may purée half or all depending on whether you prefer a smooth or rustic texture. Add whatever soup you have blended back in with the unblended part.

In a small saucepan sauté the remaining cumin seeds in the remaining oil over a moderate heat for about 1 minute, or until they are slightly crisp, and have a delicious roasted flavour. Drain onto kitchen paper.

To serve, ladle the hot lentil soup into warmed bowls, top with a tablespoon of sour cream, some coriander or mint and a sprinkling of the roast cumin seeds.

Serves 10

3 tablespoons vegetable oil

2 large onions, roughly chopped

4 cloves garlic, crushed

4 teaspoons cumin seeds

500 g (1 lb) green or brown lentils, rinsed

1 bay leaf

½ teaspoon dried oregano

3 litres (5 pints) chicken stock, water or vegetable bouillon

Garnish:

1 small tub sour cream

4 tablespoons freshly chopped coriander or mint.

hot&sour

lobster soup

Hot and sour shellfish soup from Thailand is loved and appreciated all over the world. It is normally done with prawns, but can be adapted for other fish. At first, it can be quite shocking and disorientating to the western palate, but by the end of the bowl, chances are you'll love it, and you'll have joined the converts.

2 live lobsters (approximately 625 g (1¼ lb) each)

2 tablespoons vegetable oil

2 litres (3½ pints) chicken stock

2 stalks lemon grass, crushed and chopped

1 fresh chilli, roughly chopped

1 tablespoon chopped ginger

juice and finely grated rind of 2 limes

4 Kaffir lime leaves

2 teaspoons sugar

1 teaspoon chilli paste

1 tablespoon tomato purée

salt

Garnish:

8 shiitake mushrooms, very finely sliced

2 spring onions, finely chopped

3 tablespoons fresh coriander, chopped

Boil the lobsters for 3 minutes in 4 litres (7 pints) of salted water. Remove from the pot and refresh under cold running water. Pull the tail, claws and arms from the body. With a heavy knife or lobster crackers carefully remove the meat from the arms and claws (it will still be quite raw). Squeeze the tail under a cloth until you hear it crack, then open the shell from underneath with your fingers and withdraw the tail meat. Make an incision along the length of the rounded part of the tail to expose the intestinal tract and remove and discard this. Dice all the lobster meat into 1 cm (½ inch) dice and reserve in the refrigerator.

Heat the vegetable oil in a large pot. While the oil is heating crush the lobster shells with a cleaver or mallet. When the oil is smoking, add the lobster shells and sauté, stirring frequently for 2 minutes. Now add the stock, lemon grass, chilli, ginger, lime rind, lime leaves, sugar, chilli paste, tomato purée and salt and bring to a simmer. Cook for 20 minutes, then strain into a clean pot. Allow the stock to settle for at least 20 minutes, and then carefully pour again into another clean pot leaving behind the cloudy residue.

Bring back to a simmer and finally add the lobster meat, lime juice, shiitake mushrooms, spring onions and coriander. Simmer for just 30 seconds to let the lobster meat finish cooking and then serve in warm elegant bowls.

Serves 8

(Note: if you find that you have a large amount of soft dark green matter where the lobster tail meets the body, don't dismay. You are actually lucky. This is not intestinal tract, but the coral, which is precious. It will turn bright red on final cooking.)

mussel

soup with coconut, ginger and fresh basil

Mussels with creamy coconut is one of those classic marriages. Maybe it's because they are both slightly rich and almost sweet that their flavours combine so well.

1½ kg (3 lb) live mussels

150 ml (¼ pint) white wine, dry or medium dry

4 shallots, finely chopped

1 litre (1¾ pints) canned coconut milk

½ tablespoon fresh ginger, finely chopped

3 plum tomatoes, peeled, deseeded and roughly chopped

2 large fresh chillies, deseeded and chopped

4 tablespoons cooked sweetcorn (optional)

Garnish:

1 spring onion, finely chopped

2 tablespoons fresh basil, chopped

Wash the mussels in cold running water. Pull off the hairy beard and discard any mussels which are open and therefore dead.

In a large pot boil the wine with the shallots and then add the mussels, cover and boil vigorously for 2 minutes or until all the mussels have opened. Immediately tip the mussels into a colander with a bowl underneath to catch the juice. As soon as they are cool enough to handle, carefully pull the mussels from their shells, discard any which have not opened. Reserve both the broth and the mussels.

Pour the mussel broth into a large pot, leaving behind any grit or dirt which has sunk to the bottom. Add the coconut milk, ginger, tomatoes, chillies and sweetcorn. Bring to a simmer and simmer for 2 minutes, then add the mussels. Serve in warmed bowls and finish with a sprinkle of spring onions and fresh basil.

Serves 6

corn and cheese soup with fresh

chilli

The corn soup base in this recipe is simplicity itself. It tastes wonderful without any of the spicy additions. In fact when you can get super fresh sweetcorn, do it just like that, in its purest form or with only a little chilli to taste.

Heat 1 tablespoon of the butter in a large pot over a medium heat. Add the onion and sweat for about five minutes, or until soft but without colour. Add the sweetcorn, stock and salt and bring to the boil. Simmer for 15 minutes. Purée three-quarters of the soup in a blender, and leave the rest as it is for a good rustic texture.

In a small pot, sauté the green pepper and chilli in the remaining butter, for 7 minutes. Add the tomatoes, season with a little salt and cook for 2 more minutes. Add to the corn soup.

To serve, divide the grated cheese and chives into the warmed bowls, and simply ladle the soup over the top. Serve at once, with crusty bread.

Serves 6

1½ tablespoons butter

1 medium onion,
finely chopped

450 g (14 oz) fresh sweetcorn
(frozen or tinned are
also suitable)

1½ litres (2½ pints) chicken or
vegetable stock

1 teaspoon salt, plus a pinch
for seasoning

1 small green pepper,
finely diced

2 large green chillies,
deseeded and chopped

3 plum tomatoes, peeled,
deseeded and diced

150 g (5 oz) medium
Cheddar, grated

1 tablespoon snipped chives

thai

cucumber salad

This simple salad is a delight and easy to make as most of the ingredients are always on hand. It is a great accompaniment to a main course, or as a garnish to grilled fish. The coolness of the cucumber is legendary, so enjoy this with anything spicy.

1 tablespoon fish sauce

2 tablespoons fresh lime juice

pinch of salt

1 teaspoon sugar

1 small chilli, stemmed, deseeded and chopped

grated rind of 1 lime

1 shallot, or spring onion, finely chopped

1 cucumber, peeled, deseeded and chopped

6 leaves lettuce

To garnish:

2 tablespoons salted peanuts, chopped

1 tablespoon fresh coriander, chopped

For the melon salad:

150 ml (¼ pint) coconut milk

500 g (1 lb) assorted melon, sliced or cubed

In a small bowl combine the fish sauce and lime juice. Whisk in the salt and sugar until they have dissolved, then add the chilli, lime rind and chopped shallot or spring onion. Arrange the cucumber on a bed of lettuce leaves, and pour the dressing over. Garnish with the peanuts and fresh coriander sprinkled over the top.

Serves 4

thai melon salad

This salad is nearly identical to the cucumber salad. Simply make the salad as above, but add the coconut milk to the finished dressing and replace the cucumber with the melon.

Serves 4

salads

bang bang
chicken salad

This takes its inspiration from a passion for satay and gado gado, and is just as irresistible. The coarse but smooth sauce perfectly compliments the chicken.

6 x 125 g (4 oz) boneless, skinless chicken fillets

Marinade:

1 clove garlic, finely chopped

1 tablespoon brown sugar

2 teaspoons chopped ginger

juice of ½ lime or lemon

2 tablespoons soy sauce

1 tablespoon fish sauce

pinch of hot chilli powder

1 tablespoon vegetable oil

Peanut sauce:

100 ml (3½ fl oz) peanut oil

125 g (4 oz) unsalted peanuts

2 fresh green chillies, deseeded and chopped

1 teaspoon fresh ginger

100 ml (3½ fl oz) unsweetened coconut milk, tinned or fresh

250 ml (8 fl oz) water

1 tablespoon fish sauce

2 tablespoons soy sauce

1 teaspoon brown sugar

juice of ½ lime or lemon

½ teaspoon salt

Salad ingredients:

leaves of 2 little gem lettuces

10 radishes

100 g (3½ oz) bean sprouts

3 tablespoons fresh coriander

salt and pepper

Cut each chicken fillet in half lengthwise so that you have two equal strips. Mix the marinade ingredients in an earthenware dish and add the chicken pieces. Allow to marinate for at least 1 hour.

To make the sauce, heat the oil in a heavy casserole until smoking. Add the peeled peanuts and fry for 30 seconds. Turn off the heat and allow them to finish browning slowly. After about 3-4 minutes or when browned, remove them from the oil and process in a food processor until they form a coarse purée. Add the remaining sauce ingredients and process again until the resulting sauce is coarse and grainy.

To cook the chicken, preheat your grill to high, and brush the grill tray with a little oil. Arrange the chicken strips close together but not touching in the middle of the tray, and season with salt and pepper. When the grill is very hot, cook the chicken strips on the highest shelf for about 3 minutes on each side.

To serve, arrange the salad leaves, slices or matchsticks of the radishes and the bean sprouts evenly and attractively on the plates. When the chicken has cooled slightly, cut each strip on the angle into slices. Pile the chicken on to the salad, and drizzle generously with the peanut sauce and garnish with freshly chopped coriander.

Serves 6

Note: To make it more substantial add more salad ingredients or blanched vegetables such as mangetout, carrots, broccoli or other appropriate vegetables.

wilted

spinach and smoked duck salad with chilli oil

Smoked duck and wilted spinach make this salad sound very exotic, but it can also be done with smoked ham or chicken, and with almost any other green salad leaf. The vinaigrette also works very well with grilled salmon.

To segment the oranges, cut away the skin and pith with a sharp knife. Neatly slice out the segments so that no membrane is left on the orange pieces. Catch the orange juice in a bowl while you are doing this and use for the dressing.

Combine all the ingredients for the dressing in a blender, or simply whisk them together in a bowl. Adjust the seasoning as necessary.

Bring the dressing up to the boil in a small saucepan. Pour half of it over the spinach and toss so that the leaves are coated and starting to wilt from the heat of the dressing. Divide these leaves between four warmed plates. Arrange the smoked duck and orange slices attractively on top, and garnish with a few of the spiced pecans. Drizzle a couple more tablespoons of the dressing over the top, letting it go over the smoked duck as well, and then serve immediately.

Serves 4

2 oranges

350 g (11½ oz) baby spinach leaves

1 large smoked duck breast, thinly sliced

100 g (3½ oz) spicy pecans (see recipe on page 22)

Dressing:

100 ml (3½ fl oz) vegetable oil

1 tablespoon chilli oil

2 tablespoons toasted sesame oil

50 ml (2 fl oz) fresh orange juice

25 ml (1 fl oz) fresh lemon juice

1 teaspoon honey (or sugar)

3 tablespoons soy sauce

salt and freshly ground white pepper

seared

scallop salad with avocado and spicy gazpacho

A colourful and interesting salad with loads of flavour. It is best made in late summer to get the most from the tomatoes. This recipe will give you far too much sauce, but you can either freeze it, or use it up as a soup with some crusty bread for a light lunch the next day.

Gazpacho sauce:

250 g (8 oz) unpeeled ripe tomatoes, quartered

50 g (2 oz) onion, chopped

½ teaspoon chopped garlic

½ cucumber, peeled, deseeded and chopped

1 small red pepper, cored, deseeded and chopped

150 ml (¼ pint) tomato juice

1 tablespoon sherry vinegar (or red wine vinegar)

2 tablespoons virgin olive oil

½ teaspoon salt

2 tablespoons hot chilli sauce

For the scallop salad:

600 g (1 lb 3 oz) fresh scallops

2 tablespoons vegetable oil

salt and pepper

mixed salad leaves

1 large avocado

For the vinaigrette:

salt and freshly ground black pepper, to taste

¼ teaspoon Dijon mustard

1 tablespoon white wine vinegar

4 tablespoons light olive oil

To prepare the gazpacho sauce, simply purée all the sauce ingredients in a blender. Strain through a medium sieve, and taste for seasoning, add more chilli sauce and salt and pepper as needed.

To cook the scallops, first toss the scallops in the vegetable oil and season generously with salt and pepper. Heat a heavy frying pan over a high heat until it is very hot. Add the oiled and seasoned scallops and cook until firm and just a little translucent inside (about 3 minutes each side).

To make the vinaigrette dressing, dissolve the salt and mustard with the vinegar in a bowl. Whisk in the oil and a few twists of freshly ground black pepper. Taste and adjust the seasoning as necessary.

To serve, toss the salad leaves and quartered and sliced avocado in the vinaigrette and then arrange in the centre of each plate. Surround with the spicy gazpacho sauce and place the seared scallops on top of the sauce. Serve the salad while the scallops are still warm.

Serves 4

glazed

chilli quail with bok choy

Quail is a finger-licking food and is at its best cooked on the bone. So get the extra napkins and the finger bowls ready, and go for it!

Combine all the marinade ingredients in a ceramic bowl. Toss the quail in the marinade, cover and refrigerate overnight.

To cook, preheat the grill to high. Remove the quail from the marinade and place skin side down on a baking sheet. Place under the grill on a low shelf, and cook for 5 minutes. Turn the quail over, and cook for another 5-7 minutes, basting the quail occasionally with the marinade.

Meanwhile, bring a pot of salted water to the boil and blanch the bok choy and peppers for 1 minute. Drain well and toss thoroughly in 2 tablespoons of the marinade. Arrange a bed of the vegetables on warmed plates and place the quail halves on top. Garnish with the spring onions scattered over the top.

Serves 4

4 quail, split in half through the breastbone

1 head bok choy, trimmed and sliced

½ red pepper, cut into fine strips

Marinade:

2 tablespoons dark soy sauce

2 tablespoons brown sugar

3 tablespoons chilli sauce

1 tablespoon chopped ginger

1 tablespoon sherry

1 clove garlic, crushed

2 tablespoons vegetable oil

1 teaspoon toasted sesame oil (optional)

2 spring onions, finely sliced, for garnish

starters

penne

with artichokes, sun-dried tomatoes, and a chilli garlic oil

Penne with chilli garlic oil is one of our personal favourite pasta dishes. So simple and pure, it really hardly needs anything else. However, to make it into a complete meal, don't be afraid to throw in a handful of whatever vegetables are on hand. Here we entice with artichokes and sun-dried tomatoes, but feel free to expand on this.

300 g (10 oz) jar artichoke hearts

500 g (1 lb) penne

2 tablespoons light olive oil

75 g (3 oz) sun-dried tomatoes, finely sliced

Chilli garlic oil:

6 garlic cloves, peeled

4 anchovy fillets (optional, but add a real savoury depth)

½ teaspoon salt

1 tablespoon chilli flakes

4 tablespoons light olive oil

150 ml (¼ pint) virgin olive oil

Garnish:

75 g (3 oz) grated Parmesan cheese

2 tablespoons toasted pine nuts

a few fresh basil leaves

To make the chilli garlic oil, chop the garlic and anchovies and place in a small saucepan with the salt and chilli flakes. Add 2 tablespoons of the light olive oil, and heat for about 5 minutes, until the garlic begins to soften. Allow this infusion to cool and then add the virgin olive oil. (Virgin olive oil is very delicate, and its character is changed by the heating process.)

Drain and slice the artichoke hearts into bite-sized pieces.

Bring a large pot of salted water to the boil. Add the pasta, and cook until the pasta is just al dente. Drain the pasta in a colander.

Meanwhile, in a medium frying pan sauté the artichoke hearts in the olive oil until light brown. Add the sun-dried tomatoes and cook for just 1 more minute. Toss all of the cooked vegetables with the pasta in a generous amount of the chilli garlic oil, and serve garnished with the Parmesan cheese, toasted pine nuts and basil leaves.

Serves 6

spicy leek and goat's cheese

soufflé

Soufflés are downright fun and much easier than most people seem to think. If you are careful at each stage, perfect results should follow every time. And, if they don't, at least you will have a tasty omelette and a bit more experience for the next time!

Preheat the oven to 190°C (375°F), Gas Mark 5.

Melt the butter in a saucepan and, when it starts to foam, add the leeks and cook for about 3 minutes, until the leeks are getting soft. Add the flour to the pan and mix well. Slowly add the milk, stirring continuously, and continue to stir over a medium heat until the sauce has thickened. This will take about 5-10 minutes.

Remove the pan from the heat and add the sun-dried tomato, pepper, nutmeg, cayenne, chilli, half the salt, and the egg yolks. Stir to combine and then lastly add the cheese, but reserve 1 or 2 tablespoons for sprinkling on the top of the soufflés.

Beat the egg whites with the remaining salt until stiff. Add approximately one-third of the beaten egg whites into the base mixture and stir together until smooth. Finally, gently fold in the rest of the egg whites being careful not to overmix.

Spoon the mixture into well-greased soufflé dishes and sprinkle the remaining cheese on top (you can actually hold the mixture at this point for about 1 hour in the refrigerator).

Place the soufflé dishes in a bain-marie of hot water and bake for 30 minutes for the large dish or about 15 minutes if using the smaller ones. They should be well risen, and a golden crusty brown on top. Serve immediately.

Serves 6

50 g (2 oz) butter

150 g (5 oz) leeks, washed, trimmed and finely sliced

50 g (2 oz) flour

250 ml (8 fl oz) milk

50 g (2 oz) sun-dried tomato, finely diced

pinch white pepper

pinch grated nutmeg

pinch cayenne

1 small green chilli, finely chopped (optional)

1 teaspoon salt

3 egg yolks

150 g (5 oz) goat's cheese, grated or finely crumbled

8 egg whites

1 buttered (2 litre/3 pint) soufflé dish, or 6 little ramekins (9 cm/3½ inches) diameter

devilled

oyster gratin with bacon and wilted greens

Amongst serious oyster lovers there is much heated debate whether they should be left raw and pure, or can they be cooked and spiced up a little? Well, we would urge you to try being less precious this once and try these, and simply enjoy.

20 live oysters, washed and shucked, shells and juice reserved

3 tablespoons red wine vinegar

1 tablespoon cracked black pepper

2 tablespoons butter

100 g (3½ oz) baby or young spinach, stems removed and roughly chopped

100 g (3½ oz) streaky bacon, finely sliced

1 clove of garlic, crushed or finely chopped

150 g (5 oz) coarse white breadcrumbs

pinch of cayenne pepper

½ teaspoon paprika

2 tablespoons freshly grated Parmesan cheese

2 tablespoons whole grain mustard

Wash the oyster shells and reserve 20 nicely curved halves.

Check the oysters with your fingers to make sure that there are no fragments of shell remaining. Strain the oyster juice into a small saucepan and boil over a high heat with 2 tablespoons of the vinegar and a pinch of the black pepper, until you have only 2 tablespoons of liquid remaining.

Add 1 tablespoon of the butter and bring to the boil again. Add the spinach leaves, immediately remove from the heat and allow the spinach to wilt.

In a heavy frying pan sauté the bacon strips in the remaining butter until golden brown. Add the garlic and fry for another 30 seconds. Add the remaining red wine vinegar, and allow it to sizzle and remove the pan from the heat. Lastly, add the bread-crumbs, remaining black pepper, cayenne, paprika and Parmesan cheese and mix thoroughly.

Place a little of the wilted spinach into each shell, top with an oyster and brush with mustard. Sprinkle each oyster generously with the bacon and breadcrumb mixture. Place these filled shells carefully on a baking sheet, and bake in a preheated oven 180°C (350°F), Gas Mark 4, for about 5 minutes or until nicely browned. Serve immediately by simply arranging these attractively on warmed plates.

Serves 4

salmon carpaccio with lime juice and
ginger

A great dish for adventurous eaters who don't mind some-
thing a little different. If you don't mention to your
guests that the fish is actually raw, you will almost
always find that they will eat it with great enthusiasm,
and are pleasantly surprised when they find out what
they have just eaten. You will find pickled ginger in
Asian supermarkets.

To prepare the salmon, trim the fillet of any brown meat and
check for any bones, which should be removed with tweezers or
small pliers. With a long, sharp knife, cut the fillet into 12 thin
slices. Lightly oil some clingfilm or greaseproof paper, place the
salmon slices on the clingfilm or paper and with a small rolling
pin or a cleaver lightly flatten each slice so that it is very thin
and even.

The salmon can be prepared ahead to this point and then covered
and refrigerated until needed.

To make the dressing, whisk the sugar and salt with the lemon
and lime juices in a small bowl until the sugar is dissolved. Now
add the olive oil, chilli, ginger, pepper and red onion. Whisk just
briefly to combine.

To serve, spoon the dressing evenly over the salmon on the plates
and allow to marinate at room temperature for 10 minutes..You
will notice that the salmon will change colour, and begin to
"cook" in the dressing. Finally sprinkle each plate with the fresh
coriander and a little of the chopped flower petals and serve.

Serves 6

500 g (1 lb) fresh salmon fillet
(from the head or middle)
½ teaspoon sugar
½ teaspoon salt
75 ml (3 fl oz) fresh
lemon juice
75 ml (3 fl oz) fresh lime juice
150 ml (¼ pint) light olive oil
2 large red chillies, stemmed,
deseeded and chopped
1 tablespoon very finely sliced
pickled or fresh ginger
½ teaspoon cracked
black pepper
1 small red onion,
finely chopped
Garnish:
1 tablespoon fresh coriander,
chopped
1 packet edible flowers,
roughly chopped (optional)

fish

blackened

monkfish with curried aubergine

Blackened fish is one of the most famous dishes of New Orleans. Here the technique has been adapted for the home cook. It is no less delicious, however, even if a little smokey.

700 g (1 lb 6 oz) monkfish fillets, boneless and trimmed

2 tablespoons light olive oil

Curried aubergine:

4 tablespoons light olive oil

1 large aubergine, diced

1 large onion, thinly sliced

1 fresh chilli, deseeded and chopped

1 teaspoon hot curry powder

2 tablespoons fresh coriander, chopped

salt and pepper

Blackening spices:

1 teaspoon salt

½ teaspoon oregano

½ teaspoon thyme

½ teaspoon black pepper

¼ teaspoon white pepper

¼ teaspoon onion powder

¼ teaspoon garlic powder

¼ teaspoon cayenne pepper

¼ teaspoon paprika

To make the aubergine, sauté the dices in a large frying pan over a high heat with 3 tablespoons of the oil. Cook for about 6 minutes, or until the aubergine is nicely browned and quite soft. Drain on kitchen paper.

In another pan, gently heat the remaining oil, add the onion and chilli and sauté until soft, this takes about 5 minutes. Add the curry powder and cook for 2 minutes more. Now stir in the aubergine and cook for a further 2 minutes. Finish with the fresh coriander, check the seasonings and keep warm.

For the monkfish, combine the blackening seasonings in a small bowl. Drizzle the monkfish with ½ tablespoon of the oil and all of the seasoning mix. Rub the seasoning spices into the monkfish.

Heat a large heavy frying pan over a high heat until almost smoking. Add the remainder of the oil and the monkfish fillets. Cook for 3 minutes on each side. This is a slightly smokey process, but continue cooking at a high temperature letting the seasoning "blacken". Serve immediately on a bed of curried aubergine.

Serves 4

stir-fried prawns with chilli and

basil

This is a version of a classic Thai dish which would normally be served with sticky fragrant rice. It would taste great with any variety of rice, or even pasta, so do whichever you prefer. Try to get Thai basil as it has a wonderful mystical liquorice scent which suits this dish perfectly.

400 g (13 oz) king prawns, raw

75 ml (3 fl oz) vegetable oil

2 small green chillies, deseeded and finely chopped

2 cloves garlic, finely chopped

½ red pepper, sliced

½ yellow pepper, sliced

2 large ripe tomatoes, peeled, deseeded and diced

4 tablespoons shredded basil leaves

2 tablespoons fish sauce

1 tablespoon fresh lemon juice

salt and pepper

3 spring onions, finely sliced, for garnish

Shell the prawns, leave on the tails if you prefer, for presentation. Heat the oil in a wok or large heavy frying pan over a high heat until almost smoking. Add the chillies and garlic and fry until the garlic has turned a light brown, this takes only about 30 seconds. Then add the prawns and cook for about 1 minute. Add the peppers and cook for another minute. Now add the tomato, basil, fish sauce and lemon juice. Heat through and check for seasoning. Serve immediately garnished with the spring onions.

Serves 4

salt

chilli sole with a fresh coriander aioli

Speaking from experience, people absolutely love this dish. It's so racy, versatile and satisfying. Serve it with absolutely anything, from salad to stir-fried vegetables or spicy chips.

To make the aioli, combine the egg yolks, tomato purée, garlic, vinegar, water, mustard and anchovies in a food processor or blender. Blend together, and then with the machine still running, slowly pour in the oil and process until smooth. Season with salt and pepper and add some lemon juice to taste. Add the fresh coriander, and reserve in a small bowl.

To cook the sole, heat the oil in a deep fat fryer or large saucepan to 190°C (375°F). Check that the sole fillets are dry. Cut each fillet in half on a slight diagonal. Combine the egg white and cream in a bowl, and then rub the mixture into the sole fillets so that each piece has a sticky coating. Mix together all the ingredients for the spiced flour. Cover each fillet heavily with the flour pressing it into the fish so that it coats it thoroughly and evenly. Fry the fish in two batches, draining the fillets on paper towels as they are ready. It will take approximately 2 minutes for the fillets to cook to a nice golden brown. Serve immediately on warmed plates surrounded with the aioli.

Serves 4

3 Dover sole, approximately 625 g (1¼ lb) each, skinned and trimmed

1 egg white

2 tablespoons whipping cream

Aioli ingredients:

2 egg yolks

1 tablespoon tomato purée

1 tablespoon chopped garlic

1 teaspoon white wine vinegar

1 tablespoon water

1 teaspoon Dijon mustard

2 anchovies, finely chopped

200 ml (7 fl oz) vegetable oil

salt and pepper

lemon juice, to taste

3 tablespoons fresh coriander, chopped

Spiced mixed flour mixture:

150 g (5 oz) plain flour

1½ teaspoons salt

3 tablespoons sesame seeds (black and white mixed if possible)

2 teaspoons white pepper

2 teaspoons chilli powder

2 teaspoons curry powder

oil for deep fat frying

fillet
of salmon with a horseradish crust

There is a wonderful contrast between the softness of the cooked salmon and the crisp spicy crust. This is definitely worth a go at your next dinner party.

To make the sauce, boil the cream in a saucepan for 2 minutes or until it has thickened slightly. Remove from the heat and whisk in the mustards, horseradish, lemon juice and taste for seasoning adding a little salt or lemon juice as necessary. Keep warm but do not let this boil again, or the flavours of the mustard and horseradish will be spoilt.

To prepare the salmon, check the salmon has been properly trimmed and is boneless. If there are any bones remaining remove them with a pair of tweezers. Cut the salmon into 4 equal portions. Season each piece with salt and pepper and then dredge lightly with the flour.

For the crust, mix together the horseradish and egg yolk. Dip the topside of each piece of salmon into the horseradish/egg yolk mixture, making sure that each fillet is generously coated. Mix together the breadcrumbs and fresh parsley and then dip each piece of fish into the breadcrumbs. Shape the crust by pressing on this mixture gently but firmly with your hands.

To cook the salmon, heat the oil in a heavy bottomed frying pan until very hot. Add the salmon, crust side down with the butter, and cook for 3 minutes or until the breadcrumbs are beginning to crisp up nicely. Turn the salmon over and finish off the cooking by placing in a preheated oven 180°C (350°F), Gas Mark 4, for 5 minutes.

To serve, add the chives to the sauce. Lay the salmon on a bed of buttered, cooked vegetables if you wish (spinach is great), and surround with a little of the sauce.

Serves 4

750 g (1½ lb) boneless salmon fillet

flour for dredging

salt and pepper

1 tablespoon vegetable oil

1 tablespoon butter

For the chive sauce:

250 ml (8 fl oz) double cream

1 teaspoon Dijon mustard

1 teaspoon English mustard

1 teaspoon creamed horseradish

1 tablespoon fresh lemon juice

1 tablespoon freshly snipped chives

salt and pepper

For the crust:

2 tablespoons creamed horseradish

1 egg yolk

100 g (3½ oz) coarse breadcrumbs

1 tablespoon freshly chopped parsley

peppered

tuna steak with an avocado and red onion salsa

*All over the western world foodies are raving enthusias-
tically about tuna. Not the drab tinned variety but perfect
thick steaks, quickly grilled and served medium rare.
Eating is believing.*

**600 g (1 lb 3 oz) very fresh
tuna, cut into 4 steaks**

salt

**25 g (1 oz) cracked
black peppercorns**

2 tablespoons light olive oil

Avocado and red onion salsa:

**2 tablespoons fresh lime juice
(or lemon)**

½ teaspoon salt

½ teaspoon chilli powder

6 tablespoons virgin olive oil

**2 avocados, stoned and cut
into dice**

**1 large tomato, peeled,
deseeded and cut into dice**

**¼ cucumber, peeled, deseeded
and cut into dice**

½ clove garlic, minced

1 small red onion sliced thinly

**1 tablespoon fresh coriander,
chopped**

To prepare the tuna, first trim the tuna steaks of any dark flesh,
or skin. Season the steaks lightly with salt and then coat each
steak evenly with the cracked black pepper, pressing it firmly
into the tuna steaks with your hand. Coat lightly in the oil and
refrigerate until ready to cook.

To make the salsa, first whisk the lime juice, salt, chilli powder
and olive oil together. Add the avocado, tomato, cucumber,
garlic and red onion and toss gently. Allow this mixture to sit for
at least / hour before serving to let the flavours infuse. Just
before serving add the fresh coriander.

To cook the tuna, heat a large heavy frying pan to almost
smoking over a high heat. Sear the tuna steaks for 1 minute on
each side, and then remove to warmed serving plates. Surround
with the salsa and serve immediately.

Serves 4

navarin of lamb oriental with noodles and fresh *chilli*

This is a remaking of the very satisfying French classic "navarin d'agneau". We've twisted it about a bit in the seasonings, and added some noodles, but feel free to serve it with whatever you fancy.

100 ml (3½ fl oz) dark soy sauce

3 tablespoons fresh ginger, chopped

3 tablespoons sesame oil

2 tablespoons chopped garlic

1 tablespoon white peppercorns

10 whole star anise

1½ kg (3 lb) lamb shoulder, trimmed of fat, and cut into 4 cm (½ inch) dice

4 tablespoons vegetable oil

3 tablespoons flour

1 litre (1¾ pints) water

2 large carrots, peeled and quartered

1 large onion, peeled and quartered

1 leek, split at the top and washed thoroughly

2 packets fresh thick Shanghai noodles

2 teaspoons sesame oil

4 small green chillies, deseeded

6 spring onions

3 tablespoons fresh coriander

salt and pepper

To marinate the lamb, combine the soy sauce, ginger, sesame oil, garlic, white pepper and star anise in a large non-reactive bowl. Add the lamb pieces and toss them thoroughly to coat each piece well with the marinade. Cover and leave to marinate in the refrigerator for at least 6 hours or ideally overnight.

To cook the lamb, heat the oil over a high heat and then add the lamb in batches. As the lamb browns, sprinkle it with the flour, and continue to cook for 2 minutes more. Drain the pieces in a colander as they finish browning and then place in a heavy casserole dish. Add the water, carrots, onion and leek. Bring to a simmer and skim off any excess fat or scum. Cover and cook over a low heat (or in a low oven) for approximately 1½ hours, or until the lamb is tender.

Now strain the juices through a fine sieve and again skim off any excess fat. Pick the cooked onion, carrot and leek out of the meat and pour the strained juices back on to the meat. Check the seasoning and add a little salt and pepper if needed.

Cook the noodles in 5 litres of boiling salted water for approximately 5 minutes or until soft. Drain and toss with the sesame oil. To serve, divide the noodles into warmed bowls, and place a ladle or two of the navarin on top. Finish it off by sprinkling over the chillies, spring onions and coriander, all freshly chopped.

Serves 6

meat

crispy

pork confit with a tomatillo salsa verde

Tomatillos are the perfect foil to the richness of the crispy pork. Their sharp flavour is very distinctive, but if you can't find any feel free to use green tomatoes or tinned tomatillos, which should be available from a fine food delicatessen. Failing that, try a good shop bought salsa verde.

6 x 200 g (7 oz) thick pork steaks, cut from the neck or shoulder
1 litre (1¾ pints) rendered pork or duck fat
Marinade ingredients:
6 tablespoons coarse sea salt
4 cloves garlic, roughly chopped
1 tablespoon crushed black peppercorns
2 teaspoons ground cumin
2 teaspoons dried oregano
1 tablespoon chilli powder
Salsa:
350 g (12 oz) fresh tomatillos, husked and washed
1 tablespoon chopped onion
½ teaspoon chopped garlic
1 fresh green chilli
1 tablespoon fresh lime juice
2 tablespoons olive oil
½ teaspoon salt
½ teaspoon sugar
2 tablespoons fresh coriander, chopped

To prepare the pork, place the steaks in a ceramic dish and sprinkle evenly with the marinade ingredients. Cover and refrigerate for 24 hours. The next day, warm the duck or pork fat in a heavy casserole, place the pork steaks in the melted fat, and bring to a gentle simmer. Cover and cook very slowly for 1½-2 hours, or until the steaks are very tender. Be careful when handling the steaks at this point because they will be very fragile and will break up easily.

To make the salsa, purée all the salsa ingredients, except the fresh coriander, in a blender or food processor. Add the coriander just before serving otherwise it will go grey and musty.

To prepare for serving, preheat the grill to high. Crisp the pork steaks by placing them under the hot grill for about 3-4 minutes on each side. Place on warmed plates, and garnish with the tomatillo salsa.

Serves 6

Note: this dish is super with black beans, see page 24.

chopped moroccan lamb steak with a mint

butter

Lamb with good flavour is perfect for spicy seasonings. Jazz up this classic Moroccan recipe with salad, grilled vegetables, or even simple old mashed potatoes.

1 kg (2 lb) fresh lamb pieces

4 tablespoons finely chopped onion

½ teaspoon finely chopped garlic

1 teaspoon ground cumin

½ teaspoon ground coriander seed

1 teaspoons oregano

1 teaspoon harissa

1 teaspoon black pepper

2 tablespoons chopped parsley

2 teaspoons salt

2 tablespoons vegetable oil

Mint butter:

225 g (7½ oz) unsalted butter at room temperature

3 tablespoons lemon juice

50 g (2 oz) chopped fresh mint leaves

½ teaspoon salt

freshly ground black pepper

Trim the lamb of any bones or sinews but leave on enough fat to keep it moist (10-20%). Chop it finely with a large butcher's knife or mince it coarsely. In a large bowl combine the lamb with all of the seasonings including the onion, garlic and salt. Form into 6 even-sized burgers. Heat a large frying pan over a high heat and sauté the lamb burgers in the oil for 3 minutes on each side for a pink steak and 6 minutes on each side for well done.

While the lamb is cooking combine all the ingredients for the mint butter in a food processor and blend for 30 seconds. Turn the butter into a clean bowl.

Present on warm plates with a dollop of fresh mint butter and any other accompaniment you prefer.

Serves 6

chargrilled

chicken paillard with a smoked chilli butter

Nowadays the term "paillard" refers to a thin, flat piece of meat or fish. It is cooked very quickly and looks very dramatic. Here we serve it with grilled vegetables but really it suits almost anything. An ordinary grill is just as effective as a chargrill.

To prepare the chicken paillards, lay each breast flat on a cutting board and make a long horizontal incision almost through the breast, so that you can open it out like a book. Press each breast out flat with the palm of your hand to give a good flat shape. Season each chicken piece with salt, pepper, herbs and oil. Set to one side.

To make the chilli butter, place all the ingredients in a food processor and process for 30 seconds until it is smooth and shiny. Coat the vegetables with salt and pepper and oil. Place the vegetables on a preheated very hot chargrill and cook for 1-2 minutes on each side. Remove to a warm plate while you cook the chicken.

Cook the chicken on the chargrill for approximately 4 minutes on each side, turning each after a few minutes to give a nice criss-cross effect.

To serve, place each chicken paillard in the middle of a warm plate, surround with grilled vegetables and top with a spoonful of the chilli butter.

Serves 4

4 x 150 g (5 oz) skinless chicken breasts

1 tablespoon chopped fresh herbs, parsley, rosemary, thyme

1 tablespoon vegetable oil

salt and cracked black pepper

Smoked chilli butter:

250 g (8 oz) unsalted butter at room temperature

2 tablespoons lemon juice

2 tablespoons chopped fresh herbs (as above)

2 anchovies finely chopped

1 tablespoon chopped shallots

4 tablespoons smoked barbe-cue sauce (or smoked ketchup)

2 smoked jalepeño (chipolte) chillies or fresh chillies, sliced

½ teaspoon salt

¼ teaspoon ground white pepper

Vegetables:

1 aubergine and 2 courgettes sliced 1 cm (½ inch) thick

1 yellow pepper and 1 red pepper, deseeded and cut into 8 pieces

50 ml (2 fl oz) light olive oil

salt and pepper

duck

steak "au poivre" with crispy fried vegetables

Most people love steak and chips. Well, here they have a funky twist. Duck really suits the black pepper, and the vegetables are tasty and great fun.

4 Barbary duck breasts

(approx 200 g (7 oz) each)

4 tablespoons cracked

black pepper

salt

1 tablespoon butter

1 tablespoon vegetable oil

1 tablespoon chopped shallots

1 tablespoon sherry vinegar

50 ml (2 fl oz) meat

gravy/stock

50 ml (2 fl oz) Cognac

(or brandy)

200 ml (7 fl oz) double cream

For the vegetables:

300 g (10 oz) mixed vegetables

cut into julienne strips

(eg. carrot, celeriac, potato,

leek, courgette, beetroot)

oil for deep frying

Carefully remove the skin from the duck breasts; do this by pulling the skin away from the flesh and then releasing any flesh that sticks to the skin with a sharp knife. Discard the skin. Spread the cracked peppercorns generously over the duck breasts, pressing down the pepper to encrust the duck. Season the breasts with salt. Heat the butter and oil in a large frying pan over a high flame. Fry the duck for 3 minutes on each side for medium rare or 6 minutes each side for well done. Remove the duck breasts from the pan and keep warm. Add the shallots and sherry vinegar to the pan and stir well to scrape up all the meat juices. Add the meat stock, cognac and cream and simmer until reduced to the sauce consistency preferred.

To cook the crispy vegetables, heat approximately 2 litres of vegetable oil in a large pot or a deep-fat fryer to 180-190°C (350-375°F) (test the temperature with a piece of bread; it should sizzle energetically without browning immediately). Fry all the vegetables, stirring occasionally until they stop sizzling and are crispy. Remove and drain on to a paper towel, season with salt.

To serve, cut each duck breast into slices and arrange on warm plates. Surround with a little sauce and a 'haystack' of the crispy fried vegetables

Serves 4

barbecued

t-bone steak with chargrilled potatoes

Meat cooked on the bone is simply the best. For even better results try having your T-bones cut twice as thick as you normally would.

Light the barbecue and let it get hot. If you do not have a barbecue, use your grill instead. While you are waiting, allow the T-bone steaks to come to room temperature, and then season with salt and pepper and brush with the olive oil.

To make the barbecue sauce, simply put all the ingredients into a heavy casserole and bring to a simmer over a medium heat. Turn the heat down to low, cover and cook gently for 1½ hours, stirring frequently. Remove from the heat and purée in a food processor. This keeps well in the refrigerator in an airtight container.

When the coals are hot, grill the steaks for approximately 5 minutes each side for a rare steak, or 8 minutes each side for medium to medium well done steaks. Near the end of the cooking time, paint the steaks with a little of the barbecue sauce to give them a beautiful glaze.

While the steaks are cooking, cut the potatoes in half lengthwise. Toss them in the olive oil with some salt, pepper, chilli powder and thyme. (It is important that the potatoes are a little undercooked or they will end up sticking to the barbecue.) Place them on the grill, cut side down, and let them become well marked, and nicely brown before turning them (this takes approximately 5 minutes).

Cook on the other side (skin side down) for 2 minutes and then remove them to a warm serving dish. Set aside.

When the steaks are cooked to the stage you desire, remove them and serve with the grilled potatoes, and plenty of the barbecue sauce on the side.

Serves 6

6 T-bone steaks, approx
450 g (15 oz each)
2 tablespoons cracked
black pepper
salt
2 tablespoons light olive oil
500 g (1 lb) new potatoes,
boiled in their skins
4 tablespoons light olive oil
1 teaspoon chilli powder
1 tablespoon chopped fresh
thyme (or 1 teaspoon
dried thyme)
salt and freshly ground
black pepper
Barbecue sauce:
3 tablespoons light olive oil
2 onions, roughly chopped
1 x 400 g (13 oz) tin
plum tomatoes
100 ml (3½ fl oz) tomato
ketchup
1 tablespoon garlic, chopped
100 g (3½ oz) brown sugar
100 ml (3½ fl oz) cider vinegar
200 ml (17 fl oz) water
3 tablespoons
Worcestershire sauce
1 tablespoon Dijon mustard
1 tablespoon chilli powder
½ tablespoon cumin powder

bread

spicy
corn pancakes

A wonderful option for vegetarians. You can serve these pancakes with a big spoonful of guacamole on top, or try them with grilled goat's cheese as a simple starter.

100 g (3½ oz) flour
50 g (2 oz) finely ground cornmeal
½ teaspoon baking powder
½ teaspoon baking soda
1 teaspoon salt
1 teaspoon sugar
250 ml (8 fl oz) buttermilk at room temperature
1 egg
2 tablespoons melted butter
250 g (8 oz) frozen or tinned corn kernels
3-4 serrano chilli peppers
1 tablespoon freshly chopped spring onions

Sift the dry ingredients together. Lightly whisk the buttermilk, egg and melted butter. Place half the corn kernels in a food processor, and process to a purée. Finely chop the chillies.

Add the dry ingredients to the wet ingredients and fold until just mixed. Fold in the corn purée, the kernels, chilli and spring onions. The batter should be of a pouring consistency, neither too runny nor too thick. Adjust as necessary, adding more buttermilk to thin out the mixture.

Heat a non-stick frying pan over a medium heat and ladle in the batter, making small 7 cm (3 inch) diameter pancakes. Cook for about 3 minutes on each side. Place the cooked pancakes in a low oven to keep warm while cooking the remaining batter. These are best served at once.

Makes approx 12 x 7 cm (3 inch) pancakes

ciabatta

with black pepper and fresh thyme

Everyone is familiar with this hearty loaf from Italy. The heat of the black pepper and the heady aroma of fresh thyme elevate this bread to the sublime.

8 g (¼ oz) fresh yeast
or 3½ g (⅛ oz) dried yeast
550-600 ml (17-17½ fl oz) water
1 kg (2 lb) strong flour
70 ml (3 fl oz) light olive oil
25 g (1 oz) salt
2 teaspoons cracked black pepper
4 tablespoons fresh thyme, roughly chopped

Mix the yeast in 100ml (3½ fl oz) of the water until the mixture is foamy (this takes about 5 minutes). Place the yeast/water mixture, flour, oil, salt and the remainder of the water into a mixer and mix with a dough hook for a good 5 minutes. The resulting dough should be shiny and elastic, and look quite moist in comparison to the usual bread dough. It will be sticky and this extra moisture is important.

Turn the dough into a greased bowl, cover and leave to rise until double, at least 1½ hours. (We frequently make this dough and leave at room temperature overnight and then continue the process in the morning.)

Turn the dough out onto a clean surface. Have a small bowl of flour close by to dust both the dough and your hands during the shaping process. Cut the dough into three portions and one at a time work in the following manner. Knock back the dough a couple of times first by simply lifting and slapping it down on to the work top. Combine the black pepper and thyme. Keeping 2 tablespoons of the total thyme/pepper mixture aside sprinkle about a third of the the remaining mixture over this dough. Press the mixture into the dough quite firmly with your fingers.

Pat the dough out into a flattened round, about 3-4 cm (1½-1¾ inches) thick. Holding one edge with one hand, gently pull and slap the other edge away, stretching the gluten in the dough to the maximum. There will be a point when the dough will not stretch anymore but instead begins to tear, stop here. The dough should now be in an extended oval shape. With both hands, roll this oval up, trying to mould into a tidy shape. Pat out flat and repeat the procedure. Little pieces of pepper and thyme will fall off in this shaping process, simply keep putting them back on to the dough. Now put this loaf aside on a surface sprinkled with flour, to prevent it sticking to the work surface, and cover with a

towel. Repeat the process with the other two dough portions and leave all three loaves to rise again until doubled in size, this takes about 40 minutes.

Dust two baking sheets with either flour or cornmeal. Take one loaf and on the work top again pat the loaf fairly flat with your fingertips. It should be about 3-4 cm (1½-1¾ inches) thick and feel nice, soft and pliable. Place onto the dusted baking sheet and cover again. Repeat with the other loaves. After twenty minutes the loaves will have risen again. Simply poke the top of each loaf with your fingertips a few times, sprinkle on the reserved pepper and thyme mixture and place the loaves in a preheated oven 200°C (400°F), Gas Mark 6. Spray or sprinkle the inside of the oven twice with a little water in the first five minutes of cooking to create a steamy atmosphere. The loaves should be ready after 20-25 minutes of cooking, depending on their thickness, to test tap on the bottom of the loaf. It should sound hollow when ready. Remove from the oven and cool on wire racks.

Makes 3 loaves

jalepeño
and cheddar cornmeal muffins

These spicy muffins are just the thing to serve with a big bowl of black bean soup. Of course they are just as delicious on their own, warm or cold.

Sift all the dry ingredients together into a large mixing bowl. Lightly stir the egg, butter and buttermilk together, and fold into the dry ingredients. Be careful not to mix too much or the muffins will be tough and chewy. Lastly, add the finely chopped chilli, fresh coriander and the grated Cheddar cheese.

Put a spoonful of the mixture into greased muffin moulds, fill each mould two-thirds full. Place in a preheated oven 190°C, 375°F, Gas Mark 5, for about 12-15 minutes, until golden brown. Turn out on to a wire rack to let cool. These can easily be frozen in a sealed plastic bag to have on hand at a moment's notice.

Makes 12 standard-size muffins

140 g (4½ oz) flour

115 g (3½ oz) fine cornmeal

1 tablespoon baking powder

1 tablespoon caster sugar

⅓ teaspoon salt

1 egg

30 g (1½ oz) melted butter

360 ml (12 fl oz) buttermilk at room temperature

1 jalepeño chilli

2 tablespoons fresh coriander

100 g (3½ oz) Cheddar cheese

focaccia

with fresh chillies, sweet peppers and coriander

A soft, chewy, pizza-style bread great on its own or as an accompaniment to bigger things. Use it as the base for a super zany sandwich. Feel free to add cheese or meat, or change the garnishes as the season dictates.

Bases:

40 g (1½ oz) fresh yeast
1 litre (1¾ pints) water
1½ kg (3 lb) strong flour
40 g (1½ oz) salt
4 tablespoons olive oil

Topping:

100 ml (3½ fl oz) olive oil
1 onion, sliced
1 red pepper, deseeded and sliced
1 yellow pepper, deseeded and sliced
2 red chillies, sliced finely
salt and freshly ground black pepper
1 bunch fresh coriander

To prepare the bases, dissolve the yeast in 200 ml (7 fl oz) of the water. When it is frothy, place it in a mixer with the rest of the ingredients. Mix with a dough hook for several minutes. The dough is ready when it is shiny, elastic and smooth. Place in a greased bowl, cover with clingfilm, and leave to rise until it has doubled in size, about 1½ hours.

Tip the risen dough onto a lightly floured surface, and divide into 8-10 even portions. Taking one piece at a time, roll the dough into a ball, and then with a rolling pin, take the dough into a round that is about 16 cm (6-7 inches) in diameter, and about 2½ cm (1 inch) thick. Place these rounds on to a floured baking tray, and again cover with clingfilm and leave to rise. These rounds will take only about ½ hour to rise again. While it is rising you can prepare the topping.

To prepare the topping, heat a large heavy frying pan to almost smoking, drizzle in a little oil, and sauté the onion, taking care not to let them take colour. After 2 minutes, add the peppers and continue to cook. After 3 minutes, add the chopped chillies, and season with salt and pepper. Take off the heat and reserve. Pick the coriander leaves from the bunch and set aside.

To assemble, lightly brush the top of each focaccia with a little olive oil, using the balls of your fingers, press down the centre in a dimpled manner. Place a generous spoonful of the topping in each centre, and garnish liberally all over with the coriander leaf. Place in a preheated oven, 200°C (400°F), Gas Mark 6, for 15-20 minutes, until golden brown. Remove and transfer to a wire rack, and brush lightly with the olive oil. Serve immediately!

Makes 8-10 individual size bases.

Note: Focaccia freezes well and is very handy to have on hand.

savoury chilli
bread

This loaf is just bursting with flavours. Serve as an accompaniment to soup or salad, slice thinly and toast to serve with dips, or serve on its own.

First place the yeast, water and sugar together in a small bowl and set aside for five minutes until foamy and frothy.

Meanwhile heat the oil over a medium heat. When the oil is hot, sauté the onion and red pepper until soft and translucent. Take off the heat and add the chilli and coriander. Set aside.

Place the flour, cornmeal, salt, sugar and cayenne in a mixing bowl. Stir together the buttermilk, water and melted butter. With a dough hook, work these wet ingredients, the yeast mixture and the dry ingredients together for several minutes. The dough will be fairly moist, but should come together and be firm and elastic. Form the dough into a ball and place in a greased bowl. Cover with clingfilm and leave in a warm place to rise until doubled in bulk, this takes about 1 hour.

Knock back the dough on a work surface by punching it down a few times. Now add the cooled sautéed vegetables and cheese. Grease a loaf tin and arrange the dough in the tin. Cover again with clingfilm, leave to rise until double, about 30 minutes. Bake in a preheated oven 190°C (375°F), Gas Mark 5, for 50-60 minutes, until golden and if tapped on the bottom sounds hollow. Cool on a wire rack for at least 20 minutes before eating.

Makes 1 loaf

20 g (¾ oz) fresh yeast

100 ml (3½ fl oz) water

1 teaspoon sugar

1 tablespoon oil

¼ red onion, finely chopped

½ red pepper, finely chopped

4-6 serrano chilli peppers,
very finely chopped

3 tablespoons chopped
fresh coriander

550 g (1 lb 1 oz) flour

100 g (3½ oz) fine cornmeal

½ teaspoon salt

2 tablespoons sugar

¼ teaspoon cayenne pepper

125 ml (4 fl oz) buttermilk

125 ml (4 fl oz) water

4 tablespoons melted butter

150 g (5 oz) grated cheese,
Cheddar or Monterey Jack

desserts

peppered **strawberries**

A simple yet zesty way with strawberries which will both surprise and please the palate.

750 g (1½ lb) strawberries, hulled and halved

2 tablespoons caster sugar

1½ tablespoons Grand Marnier

1½ tablespoons Kirsch

freshly ground or cracked black pepper

Garnish (optional):

a few mint leaves

icing sugar

Simply marinate the strawberries in the sugar and liqueurs for about 15 minutes. The sugar may need adjusting depending on the natural sweetness of the berries. Just before serving, sprinkle as generously as your taste permits with the freshly ground black pepper. Garnish with mint leaves and icing sugar if you wish

There are several ways of serving this dish. Once marinated the strawberries go beautifully with fresh vanilla ice cream, piled high in a sundae dish. Another idea is to take softly whipped cream, fold in an equal quantity of puréed strawberries, and fold the marinated peppered berries together with this mixture to create a tasty fool-type dessert.

Serves 6

Note: Be sure not to marinate the berries too long. They will go very soft and soggy, and lose their fresh fragrance and flavour. And remember not to add the pepper until serving time. The flavours meld together in surprising harmony, and will delight friends and family.

refreshing

ice cream with a wicked fudge sauce

The pure unadulterated flavours of fresh ginger and dark chocolate go together like peas in a pod.

125 ml (4 fl oz) water
250 g (8 oz) sugar
125 g (4 oz) fresh ginger, chopped
500 ml (17 fl oz) full fat milk
500 ml (17 fl oz) whipping cream
10 egg yolks
For the fudge sauce:
250 g (8 oz) dark chocolate, chopped
100 g (3½ oz) butter
125 g (4 oz) sugar
150 ml (¼ pint) whipping cream
1 teaspoon good quality vanilla extract
pinch salt

Put the water and 100 g (3½ oz) of the sugar in a small pot and bring to the boil. Add the chopped ginger and simmer gently for 5 minutes.

Place the milk and cream in a medium saucepan and bring to the boil. Add the ginger/sugar syrup and leave it to infuse off the heat for a good 20-30 minutes. Gently bring back up to its boiling point.

Whisk the remaining sugar with the egg yolks until the sugar is well dissolved, and then while still whisking, pour on the boiled milk/cream mixture. Pour it all back into the saucepan and, stirring continuously, cook over a gentle heat until the mixture has thickened to a custard consistency (about 7 minutes). Strain through a fine meshed sieve, and let cool.

Once chilled, this custard can be turned, according to your manufacturer's instructions, in an ice cream machine.

To make the fudge sauce, combine the chocolate, butter, sugar and cream in a bowl, place the bowl over a hot but not boiling saucepan. Stir occasionally until melted. Do not let the water in the under pot boil because it will give the chocolate a burnt taste. Stir in the vanilla and salt and keep in a warm place until needed. This sauce can be reheated in a microwave or saucepan and will keep in the fridge for about a week.

To serve, place several scoops of this delicious ice cream in individual serving bowls, and drizzle generously with the hot fudge sauce.

Serves 4-6

citrus
sabayon

*This sabayon can be an accompaniment to poached fruit
or a dessert by itself in the same manner as that classic
Italian dessert, zabaglione. If you want to serve it cold,
simply fold in softly whipped cream after you have
chilled it. Utterly refreshing any way.*

Whisk the yolks and sugar together in a medium-sized stainless steel bowl. Add the lemon and lime rind, ginger and wine and place over a pot of barely simmering water. Whisk constantly until it begins to thicken and continue to whisk until it has doubled in volume, (this takes about 10 minutes). Taste and add a few drops of lemon or lime juice if it needs a bit more acidity. This can be served immediately as a warm sauce.

To make into a cold sauce or a dessert in its own right, place the bowl over an ice bath (ice cubes and water in a bigger bowl than the one the sabayon is in). Continue to whisk gently until it has cooled completely. If you do not whisk continuously at this stage all the volume achieved in the cooking process will disappear. Once it has cooled completely, fold in the cream. It should not be too firmly whipped, just at the soft peak stage. This looks beautiful in tall glasses garnished with a bit of sugared lemon or lime peel, crystallized ginger and mint.

Serves 6

6 egg yolks

125 g (4 oz) sugar

**1 tablespoon finely grated
lemon and lime rind (mixed)**

½ teaspoon ground ginger

**225 ml (7½ fl oz) crisp dry
white wine**

**2 tablespoons lime and/or
lemon juice, as needed**

**225 ml (7½ fl oz) double cream,
whipped (optional)**

Garnish (optional):

sugared lemon or lime peel

crystallized ginger

mint leaves

drinks

sangria

Sometimes a meal has so many flavours that you can be quite lost at having to choose a wine. A wonderful option is this sangria, a lightened-up version of a glass of wine, which can hold its own against the spicier foods. Imagine a balmy summer evening, the barbecue in full swing, friends are dropping in... Your guests will love it.

Pour all of the liquids into a large capacity jug or bowl. Then add the sugar and stir all of the ingredients together until completely dissolved. Add all of the fruit to the mixture and then chill in the refrigerator for at least one hour. Serve with plenty of ice cubes in tall glasses.

Makes about 2 litres (3 pints)

1 litre (1¾ pints) full dry
red wine
1 litre (1¾ pints) sparkling
mineral water
200 ml (7 fl oz) fresh
lime juice
50 ml (2 fl oz) Grand Marnier,
or other orange liqueur
200 g (7 oz) sugar
1 orange, sliced
1 lemon, sliced
2 peaches, skinned and sliced

chai

We find this spiced tea, shared with us by a friend from Goa very refreshing, soothing and relaxing. Feel free to alter the spices to your own tastes, more cinnamon, less cardamom, and so on.

Simply put all the ingredients into a medium saucepan, and bring to the boil. Immediately reduce the heat so that it is barely simmering. Leave to simmer for about 20-30 minutes and then strain into warmed cups. Offer more sugar as personal taste dictates.

Serves 6

1 litre (2 pints) water
1½ teaspoons Darjeeling tea,
loose
150 ml (¼ pint) milk
30 g (1 oz) sugar
¼ cinnamon stick, about
6-8 cm (2 inches)
½ teaspoon whole green
cardamoms, crushed open
½ teaspoon freshly
grated ginger

californian

margarita

75 ml (5 fl oz) Cuervo Gold
tequila
75 ml (5 fl oz) Grand Marnier
liqueur
250 ml (8 fl oz) freshly
squeezed lime juice
6-8 tablespoons caster sugar
300 ml (½ pint) ice cubes
You will also need:
4 martini-style glasses (any
attractive stemmed glass
will suffice)
shallow bowl of salt
4 slices of lime
4 lime leaves (optional)

This is a snazzy, up-beat version of an old classic cocktail that was developed while bartending in a singles bar in Calgary, Canada.

Simply place all of the ingredients in a blender and process quickly. The ice should turn to a slushy consistency. Adjust the sweetness as desired (as with all fresh fruit the natural sweetness of the limes will vary). Run a slice of lime around the rim of each glass and dip the rim into a shallow bowl of salt to achieve a crusty rim of salt. Carefully pour the slushy cocktail into each glass. Garnish with a slice of lime and lime leaf, if you wish, and enjoy! These go down amazingly well so have the ingredients ready for seconds.

Serves 4

southern comfort cocktail

500 ml (17 fl oz) good quality
pineapple juice
100 ml (3½ fl oz) fresh
orange juice
100 ml (3½ fl oz) apple juice
100 ml (3½ fl oz) Southern
Comfort
slices of orange and pineapple
for garnish (optional):

Usually we would ask for an ice cold Asian beer to down with any Mexican, Indian, Thai or Chinese meal that promised loads of red hot spice and fire, but some occasions call for that something a little bit special. This cocktail is based on Southern Comfort and pineapple juice and was introduced to us by an old friend from Winnipeg.

Simply shake or blend all the ingredients together. Fill 4 tall glasses with ice cubes and pour over the mixture. Slices of orange and pineapple are a lovely garnish.

Serves 4

lassi

During our year in India we gorged daily upon this refreshing and healthy drink. Somehow the yogurt tempers the fieriness of spicy food, making lassi an excellent accompaniment to any hot meal. There are numerous flavours, all tasty and pleasing, but a simple citrus one like this doesn't interfere with a meal's flavours.

Simply place all the ingredients into the blender and whiz up. Serve over ice cubes in tall glasses. Simple and delicious.

Serves 4-6

400 g (13 oz) plain low fat yogurt

275 ml (9 fl oz) cold water

2 tablespoons fresh lemon juice

2 tablespoons fresh lime juice

2 tablespoons fresh orange juice

3 tablespoons caster sugar

ice cubes

bloody
caesar

A refreshing and stimulating drink. The celery salt and lime compliment the spice, the celery offers a cool note.

Use a slice of lime to rub around the top of each of the glasses. Dip this moistened lip into the bowl of salt so that an even coating of salt rims the glass. Place several ice cubes in each glass and pour the vodka over. Add the clamato juice, and according to your taste, several drops each of the Worcestershire and Tabasco sauces, go slowly with the latter. Add a good shake of salt and freshly ground pepper, and stir. Arrange a slice of lime on the rim of the glass, and garnish with a stick of celery.

Serves 4

Note: Clamato juice is a mixture of clam and tomato juice. It is lighter and more savoury than pure tomato juice. Either are fine if you have trouble locating it in a local deli or fine food shop.

1 lime, sliced

shallow bowl of salt

ice cubes

4 x 40 ml (1½ fl oz) premium vodka

4 x 125 ml (4 fl oz) clamato juice (see note below)

Worcestershire sauce

Tabasco sauce

celery salt

black pepper

4 sticks raw celery, washed and trimmed for garnish

index